The International Book of

Beer Can Collecting

The International Book of

Beer Can Collecting

Richard Dolphin

CASTLE BOOKS

frontispiece
A can for the United States'
bi-centennial year 1976, by
the Lucky Brewing Co. of
San Francisco

Published in the USA by Castle Books
Distributed to the trade in the USA by
Book Sales Inc.,
110 Enterprise Avenue
Secaucus
New Jersey 07094

© The Hamlyn Publishing Group Limited 1977

ISBN 0-89009-117-X
Library of Congress Catalog Card No. 77-71297

Filmset in England by Filmtype Services Limited, Scarborough
Printed in Hong Kong
by Lee Fung—Asco Printers Limited

Contents

The beer can boom

Beer can collecting first began in the United States at the end of the 1930s. The first can appeared in 1935 and by the end of that decade there were several collectors in California and probably elsewhere. These West Coast collectors had no contact with one another; indeed it is not recorded whether they were even aware that other people were collecting cans. Very probably each thought that he was the only collector in existence.

This isolation was experienced by many individuals in different parts of the United States for more than 30 years. Even as late as the middle 1970s people collecting beer cans were amazed to discover that there were other collectors. Until the various collecting organizations sprang to life in the 1970s there was no recognized way for ordinary people to make contact with others sharing the same hobby.

Formal contacts between collectors began in the early part of the 1960s. At that point, there was no suggestion that the hobby should be organized and these early meetings were simply opportunities for collectors to meet together, establish friendships, drink a glass of beer and exchange cans. In those early days very little 'calculated' exchanging (or trading) went on — it was more usual for a collector to give a friend a selection of cans that he needed, in return for a similar gift.

As we have seen, there were beer can collectors as soon as there were beer cans, at least in the United States, but there is no evidence to suggest that collecting was established in any other country until the middle 1970s. By then it had spread to Australia, Japan, and a number of European countries.

Yet why should anyone have wanted to collect beer cans in the first place? Most enthusiasts would reply 'because beer cans are beautiful'; and so, in fact, they are. But the origins of the hobby stem more from an American passion for collecting breweriana than from an eye for beauty: the advent of the can in 1935 merely provided one more brewery item to add to the collection.

Many Americans have bars in their back rooms or basements and they found that rows of cans above the bar or on a shelf next to the bar added greatly to the overall effect. It was not really until the very late 1950s that any great attention was paid to the quality of packaging. By that time breweries around the world were spending some considerable effort on improving their can designs and by then some containers certainly could be said to be beautiful. Furthermore, they had begun to reflect the society they were made for, and changing trends in design patterns generally.

By the late 1960s there were several hundred collectors scattered across the United States, but still only a few knew of each other. Then, in October 1969, the tide turned and started running very hard in the hobby's favour. For

McEwan's of Edinburgh produced their India Pale Ale in one of Britain's first cone tops

in that month beer can collecting became known internationally and an organization was established.

During the fall of 1969, the *St Louis Globe Democrat* ran a feature on a collection of full cans of beer owned by Denver M. Wright Jr, a St Louis business executive who had been collecting for some years. There is no doubt that at that time (and possibly still) Mr Wright owned the largest collection of full cans of beer in the world. This was the first known occasion that a newspaper had featured a beer can collection and the story aroused considerable interest in St Louis and the surrounding districts.

At least six other beer can collectors read that story and each was excited to discover that there was at least one other collector in his home area. None knew of the others' collections – although most unusually the sixth reader was Denver Wright's brother, Larry Wright! The result of this article was that these men contacted each other by telephone and agreed to meet as soon as possible. Within a few days the historic gathering took place at Denver Wright's home.

None of the seven men present realized how significant or far reaching the meeting was to be. They can little have imagined that from their discussions was to arise the fastest growing hobby of the 1970s. Nonetheless, Denver Wright Jr, Tony Bruning, Bob Eckert, Glen Doran, Ken Fanger, Ray White and Larry Wright began to meet fairly often. Their social meetings turned into forums where the latest can issues were discussed and cans exchanged. Before Christmas 1969 it was suggested that a

new club should be formed, to develop the hobby nationally (and eventually internationally), and it was decided to call the club Beer Can Collectors of America.

BCCA was inaugurated on the 15th April 1970 with the expressed aim of encouraging the collection of beer cans. The club was started at a meeting held in Denver Wright's home and Mr Wright was elected the first President. The principal offices were filled by Robert Eckert (Secretary) and Kenneth Fanger (Treasurer); Larry Wright was Vice President and succeeded his brother to the Presidency a year later.

BCCA was originally devised as a small organization to help members expand their collections by trading with each other. Their addresses were given in a membership rosta, which enabled them to contact one another. In the long run the friendships that developed through membership of the club have probably outweighed all other advantages many times over.

The original membership fee was $5.00 a year and one of the first conditions of membership was that each member should file a list of all the cans in his collection. From this information a composite list was built up of all cans known to exist throughout the world. Members received the membership rosta, a membership card, BCCA stationery stickers and a copy of the composite list.

The original concept of BCCA was not particularly ambitious. The early members could hardly have foreseen that by 1977 the membership would number well over 10,000, spanning many countries on the globe. In time the orig-

Harking back to the German brewing tradition: Busch Bavarian (US), Alpine Ayingerbrau (brewed in UK), Edelweiss, Bergheim, Old German and Kodiak Cream Ale (US)

inal aims of the club would become outdated, its back-up services inadequate and the club more impersonal. But its family spirit and essential good humour have never been destroyed, despite the club's growth and the many types of people who have come into it.

Until 1974 the growth of beer can collecting was synonymous with the growth of BCCA. At the end of 1970 BCCA had only 30 members but from then on it grew in leaps and bounds. A year later membership numbered 304; it passed 1,000 in 1973 and 3,000 in 1974; by the end of 1976 it was around 10,000. Without the club and the organization and promotion it provided, the new hobby would almost certainly never have become known on as large a scale as it is now.

From September 24–26, 1971, BCCA staged the very first national show for beer cans and beer can collectors. It was held at the Holiday Inn South in Sunset Hills, Missouri, and 20 rooms were reserved for attending members. The gathering was attended by 232 people, of whom 60% were members and the rest friends. During this unique gathering Lew Cady of Denver, Colorado, earned his place in history

Five elegant 45 cl cans from Sweden

by suggesting that the next and subsequent shows should be called *can*ventions: it was so agreed and the first canvention was held the following year at Lake Geneva, Wisconsin.

By 1971, when the club was over a year old, it was no longer a condition of membership that all members had to send in lists of their cans on joining. During that year the habit was introduced of giving new members a badge inscribed 'Don't kick the can', which soon became BCCA's motto. New members were also given a windscreen sticker and blazer badge, both bearing the BCCA motif. Each member attending a canvention was also given a free commemorative can as a souvenir.

A measure of the growth of BCCA during this time was the media coverage given to members and their collections: by 1973 news of this fast growing hobby was spreading very quickly indeed. Many collectors had their displays featured in local papers and this brought other collectors in to join BCCA and at the same time encouraged more people to start collections and join in this unusual hobby.

Members were given new incentives to improve the quality of their displays, and 1972

Gränges of Sweden decorate their Export Beer III with reproductions of famous paintings

11

Canning for the fun of it: cartoons from Scandinavia and Australia

above right
Courage of Australia brew 'for expert drinkers'

saw the introduction of awards at the canvention for collector of the year, US can of the year, best overall display, best foreign display, best US flat top display, best US cone top display and best chapter display. These awards stimulate keen competition, but just as much desired was a kiss from Miss Beer Can, who was first elected in 1972 and has been prominent ever since.

The annual canventions have come to play a vital part in the growth of the hobby and are the highlight of the year for collectors, who travel from all over the United States to join in the fun. The comradeship they inspire and the knowledge they impart to collectors are as valuable as the opportunity they provide for them to expand their collections.

The canventions are like nothing on earth. On paper they are well-ordered affairs where

GENERAL GEO. WASHINGTON AND CONTINENTAL TROOPS CROSSING DELAWARE RIVER

MINIFUT 16 demis "pression"

PELFORTH Pale

LA BIERE BLONDE DE FRANCE

DANS UNE CAVE BIEN FRAICHE 24 HEURES AVANT SA MISE EN PERCE. CELLE-CI S EFFECTUERA

AMERICAN-STYLE BEER

This Malt Filtered Clear Beer is dedicated to the good name of President James Madison (1751-1836) who battled to protect the great American beer brewing tradition.

MADISON

Louis Luyt Breweries.

340ml 340ml

collectors meet to exchange cans and gossip. In reality they are large noisy meetings where trading goes on in hotel rooms, in elevators, on stairs, in parking lots – in fact any place where people find space to look at each other's cans. Enthusiasts seldom eat or sleep, but spend most of their time in a mad rush for cans which goes on well into the early hours of the morning and sometimes right through the night.

In March 1971 BCCA launched its *News Report*. This is perhaps the most valuable contribution the club makes for its ordinary members. Published every two months, its excellently produced contents are essential reading for all serious collectors, and the magazine helps in bringing members together. But as the club grew bigger it was realized that further action was required to ease the problems created by the infrequency of national meetings.

Pelforth's Pale Ale is sold in France emblazoned with Pieter Brueghel's masterpiece *The Wedding Dance in the Open Air*

opposite bottom, above left and left
Toasting the American Revolution: Valley Forge (US), Ortlieb's portrait of Washington crossing the Delaware (US) and Madison, from Luis Luyt Breweries in South Africa

13

In 1972 the first local chapter was formed in Wisconsin and this was shortly followed by the Gateway Chapter in St Louis. By 1977 most states had at least one chapter, and more in areas densely populated by collectors, as for instance around Chicago, St Louis and Dayton, Ohio.

Of course, not all members attend meetings, so another effect of BCCA's growth was the development of trading by post. Two collectors would agree to exchange particular cans and each would then mail his cans to the other. This development has been helped enormously by the BCCA membership rosta, which is up-

dated as often as possible and contains each member's name, age, occupation, address, telephone number and wife's name. The approximate size of the collection is indicated by a grading system.

The grading system is based on the use of asterisks. One * indicates a collection of between 100 and 249 cans, ** 250–499, *** 500–749, **** 750–999 and *****, the *cordon bleu* of beer can collectors, over 1,000 cans. Collectors are allotted titles by the same means, * being a 'Brewery Worker', ** an 'Apprentice Brewer', and so forth up to *****, 'Grand Brewmaster'.

Two groups of cans with animal themes:
Hall & Woodhouse Badger Stout (UK), Schell's Golden 16 and 12 oz cans (US), Black Horse (US) and Holsten Pilsener (Germany) Pripps Falcon Lattol (Sweden), Buffalo Premium Lager (US), Rogue Longbrew (South Africa), Schlitz Malt Liquor and Mustang Premium Malt Liquor (US)

14

The system works well, but is out of date now, as so many collectors have over 1,000 cans— 3,000 or more is not unusual. Too many people now qualify for the highest accolade.

The rosta also gives very much useful information on how to restore damaged cans, how to remove dents and how to preserve cans so that they remain in mint condition. It instructs members how to conduct themselves when making trades, particularly important when trading by post. It suggests how to value one type of can in relation to another, in order to arrive at the fairest possible means of exchanging.

While it is right to give much of the credit to BCCA for the formidable growth of beer can collecting, some credit lies elsewhere. As the great swell of enthusiasm for the hobby was building up in mid-1974 it became obvious that an organization with a wider base was needed, to provide collectors with easier ways of getting cans than BCCA was willing to allow. The great stumbling block was that BCCA had an obsessive dislike of collectors adding to their displays by any means other than trading. Many collectors wished to buy cans outright and BCCA disapproved of this.

above
**Fresh and natural – that's
Hop'n Gator (US)**

right
**Scandinavian drinking
heroes: A city gent on Bass
English export beer, and
comic Vikings from Röde
Orm (Sweden) and Albani
Fad (Denmark)**

far right
**WWBCC's first anniversary
can, 1975**

In 1974 several energetic people found a way for collectors to buy and sell openly without incurring the disapproval of BCCA (who will still not allow cans to be bought and sold openly at any of their meetings). Robert Dabbs and David Harris started World Wide Beer Can Collectors in Independence, Missouri, and this organization has gone from strength to strength. WWBCC publishes a monthly newsletter which is without doubt the largest beer can trading medium in existence. Membership of the organization brings one the newsletter each month and puts one in touch with other collectors all around the world who wish to exchange cans by trading, buying or selling.

This is mainly a subscription service although the club does stage quite a number of shows in well-placed regional centres in the Mid West of the United States. In addition, it puts on a national show each July which attracts increasingly large numbers of people. The Saturday night of the show is marked by a banquet, normally with a guest speaker.

This and other small and more localized organizations have helped establish such a ready market for cans that most flea markets and antique shops now sell cans – often at rather inflated prices! The beer can has in recent years become a highly prized and much valued article. The way things are going it looks as though it will remain that way for a very long time to come.

Early days

No one knows for sure who first thought of putting beer into cans. Nor are we certain when it was first tried experimentally, although two brewers, Anheuser-Busch and Pabst, both experimented with cans in 1929. This was during Prohibition, when the sale of alcoholic beverages was forbidden in the United States, but we do not know why they took the matter no further. Probably hazards of trying out a new container were considered too great to be worth taking; besides, the process was initially expensive.

In the early 1930s, however, the can manufacturing companies sought to convince the brewers that their product was a finer container for packaging beer than the bottle. In reply, the bottle makers insisted that their package was the only one in which beer could be delivered safely, with no possibility of contamination. A bottle could be used many times if it remained unbroken, while a can was only used once. They pointed out that the bottle was cheaper to use anyway, because brewers would need to buy expensive capital equipment if they turned to cans.

The can makers, very much on the offensive, counter-claimed that their container would produce a finer tasting beer. Furthermore, a lot of expensive bottle washing equipment could be done away with. Also, cans would be easier to stack than bottles, and they would take up less space. The can makers then pointed out that the deposit on a bottle involved costly paperwork and administration. They also proved that more cans could be filled in a normal working day.

When all was said and done, the main hurdle the can companies faced was not selling the basic idea, but convincing brewers and drinkers alike that the lining of the can would preserve the taste of the beer. The three major companies, American Can, Continental Can and National Can were all working independently to find satisfactory solutions to this problem. American Can(CanCo) got there first.

In 1933 Prohibition ended, and the same year Gottfried Krueger Brewing Company of Newark, New Jersey, produced a beer containing 3·2% alcohol in a can made by CanCo under the label Krueger's Special Beer. The filled 2000 cans for a private test run. It was a success and so on September 25, 1934, CanCo trademarked

their lining and patented it under the name 'Keglined'. The cans carried notices claiming that the contents were better because the goodness was sealed in and the flavour preserved.

On January 24, 1935, Krueger offered two brands of canned beer–Kreuger's Finest Beer and Krueger's Cream Ale–in a special test market staged at Richmond, Virginia. Krueger, who were a very small company, agreed to be the guinea pigs because CanCo undertook to pay all the costs of installing the necessary equipment. Krueger, however, agreed to repay all the overheads if the canned beer went well.

In the event, sales figures were beyond everybody's wildest dreams. The new packages did so well that by the early summer Krueger was taking a great deal of business from Anheuser-Busch, Pabst and Schlitz–the three major national brewers. In fact, within five months the company was running 550% of its pre-can production.

opposite
Perhaps the world's rarest can: Simonds salute the coronation of King George VI (1937)

The Krueger Co. of Newark, New Jersey, sold the first canned beer in 1935. This is one of their original cans — a flat top

Schlitz of Milwaukee broke new ground in America in 1935 with their new style of can, the cone top

While all this was going on, other brewers were watching Krueger closely and before long the Northampton Brewing Company in Northampton, Pennsylvania, followed with their Tru Blu Ale and Tru Blu White Seal Beer in containers made for them by National Can. The first national giant to issue a can was Pabst, who marketed an Export brand in July 1935. This was tried in a test run in Rockford, Illinois. Significantly, they did not package their famous Blue Ribbon brand leader in cans for some while,

so that the name would not be injured if the experiment failed.

The first cans issued in America were 'flat tops'. They were similar to those made today but had an unbroken flat top, as opposed to the modern can which has a ring tab in the top that can be ripped off. The early cans had to be opened with a special gadget for punching holes – known in the States as a 'church key'. In the first 11 months of canned beer packaging in the United States 23 different brands were issued in

The first British can: a cone
top from Llannelli's
Felinfoel Brewery

cans and of these 17 were flat tops.

On July 28, 1935, a law was introduced in the United States that each container had to bear the initials IRTP, for Internal Revenue Tax Paid. This imprint lasted until March 1, 1950, when it was abolished. Cans bearing these initials may usefully be identified as to date of origin within a 15 year period.

Schlitz caught the eye in September 1935 by issuing a new style of can. The problem with the container CanCo devised and Krueger tested

was that the brewer had to install new equipment. This meant heavy capital expense which few smaller brewers had the resources to contemplate. Continental Can designed a package that had the advantages of the flat top but was easier to market. It looked like a metal bottle, with a round body and a conical top sealed with a crown cork just like that on a bottle. Because of the conical top it was dubbed 'cone top' or 'spout top'.

The advantages of this design were twofold.

21

Simonds S.B. Pale Ale, another of the very first British issues produced in 1936

The can *looked* like a bottle, thus perhaps helping to break down consumer resistance to drinking beer from a metal container; also it was *filled* like a bottle and could be sealed with a bottle top, so brewers needed far less new equipment. In fact the first cans used outside the United States were all cone tops.

For the consumer, there was an advantage and a disadvantage. The can was easier to open than the flat top, as most drinkers already possessed bottle openers. But the cone top simply looked unattractive: in fact it resembled a tin of metal polish. In any event, these cans looked so unusual that they stayed in the memory more easily than the flat tops which came before them and to this day many people think they were the forerunners in can design.

It soon became obvious around the world that the Americans were on to a good thing and it was not long before the first European can was issued – in the most unlikely place. The Felinfoel Brewery at Llanelli, Wales, which is still in business today, produced the first canned beer outside the United States. The reason for Felinfoel being the leader in the United Kingdom was that the local tinplate industry had spare capacity which could be used to develop a new container. Felinfoel issued their Pale Ale in cone tops which were actually filled in December 1935 and marketed in January 1936. Felinfoel Ale was sold in both 9 oz and 12 oz cans before the war and a very few specimens of these cans still exist–a mint specimen would be highly valued by any collector.

The idea of canned beer was slow to catch on in the United Kingdom, perhaps because of consumer resistance. However, by May 1936, Simonds Brewery at Reading was canning Simonds Beer and Simonds S.B. Pale Ale. Then in 1937 they filled Coronation Brew in a mauve cone top, bearing the royal crown, which today is one of the world's rarest cans. Hammerton's, who were eventually swallowed by Watney's, were also canning in a 9 oz cone top before the Second World War. So also were McEwan's in Scotland, who also filled their Export in a 12 oz container for sale overseas. Jeffrey's was probably the only other Scottish brewer to produce a 9 oz cone top.

Elsewhere around the world the cone top was regarded as the norm for quite some number of years. Eleven countries are known to have produced them, and there may have been more. Cone tops were certainly issued in Belgium, Canada, England, Germany, Holland, the Isle of Man, Mexico, Scotland, the United States, Venezuela and Wales. Many collectors place great importance upon them, and would rather have a mint cone top than any other can.

The tin plate manufacturers were going to great lengths in both the United Kingdom and the United States, and later in other countries, to persuade the drinking public to accept the beer can. Success was more rapid in the United States where the new form of packaging was proving very popular as early as 1936. As more consumers expressed willingness to drink from cans, more brewers agreed to have the necessary equipment installed. The lesson of Krueger spread far and wide–for within 20 weeks of starting to can they had been unable to keep up with demand.

Americans like drinking beer and it soon became obvious that a larger can was needed to accommodate the demands of some drinkers. In 1937 a quart cone top, designed and made by Crown, Cork and Seal, was introduced; Continental produced a similar size. This larger can was particularly useful when people drank together and in some senses it could be called the first party can. Shortly afterwards American Can produced a quart flat top.

In 1937 Schlitz, early trail blazers with the cone top, abandoned it for the flat tops. Although the cone top continued to be very popular for about 20 years Schlitz had sounded its death knell. The flat top was quite simply

more efficient. The equipment was expensive, but the outlay was recouped later in savings on overheads. The manufacturers were quite aware that the days of the cone top were numbered and by 1938 the company that introduced the cone–Continental–was making flat tops. The Old Dutch Brewery in Brooklyn, New York, was the first to use them.

When the Second World War broke out in

The first German cone top: Export Bier (1937)

1939, the can was fairly well established in the United States, but in Europe it was still very much of a novelty. Just as the idea was beginning to catch on, the war halted production of beer cans for the European homemarkets and no more were made until the early 1950s. This was unfortunate for the can manufacturers, for much of their investment in marketing and publicity went to waste. The Americans were somewhat more lucky: their production was stopped for only four years.

Champagne Velvet and
Goetz Country Club (US)

Flat tops soon dominated
the can market: Pabst Old
Tankard and Ruppert
Knickerbocker (US)

From steel to aluminium

The Second World War had a devastating effect on the canning industry in Europe, but while canning for the domestic market had stopped, it continued apace for overseas markets, particularly for troops serving abroad. Quite a few UK brewers produced 12 oz cans for export during this period; for some this was the only canning they ever did.

The Castletown Brewery in the Isle of Man produced two cone tops during the period 1943–1947, both for export to overseas NAAFIs: Blue Label mild ale and Red Label pale ale. During this period the Northampton Brewery also canned for the first and only time, while McEwan's Export was another beer brewed in large quantities for troops abroad.

The United States did not enter the war until 1942, and before that another interesting development took place. The Crowntainer appeared in 1940: it was a new style of cone top. Schmidt's were the first to use this fascinating innovation, which was a two-piece can. The original cone tops had been three-piece constructions with a base, a main body and a cap. The Crowntainer had only one seam rather than two, so it reduced by half the chance of beer leaking away.

Invented by Crown, Cork and Seal, the new can was made of tinless black plate covered with powdered aluminum and had a permanent glazed appearance. The design was only five inches high, shorter than previous cones, but the strangely shaped spout was longer than in other cones. The short, stubby can was wider than normal and stacked better.

Quart and 12 oz cones had already been used when Krueger added the 16 oz cone to the range in 1941. By that year 37% of the brewers in the United States were using cans, which in turn accounted for 14% of the packaged beer sales. But the clouds of war were descending on the United States and in 1942 canning for the domestic market ceased for four years.

However, production of canned beer continued apace for US servicemen overseas, resulting in the introduction of a unique hybrid –the camouflaged can. This was a normal can, but its usual label was disguised by coloring it olive green. Over 20 such cans are known to have been issued–all Crowntainers.

opposite
Greenhall Whitley's Carnival – an attractive example of the postwar party cans (UK)

Three postwar cone tops. Krueger's Finest Beer was produced in a Crowntainer with a powdered aluminium finish

The changing face of Iron City Beer, as the Pittsburg Brewery adopted the new snap-top

below
Early British flat-tops: Simonds Golden Dry and the Hull Brewery's Export Beer

below right
Munich's famous Löwenbräu appeared in an early aluminium cone top (1950)

The war helped considerably to convert ordinary men and women to drinking beer from cans. Servicemen abroad accepted the can as a perfectly normal container and this was particularly true of the younger men who started drinking while abroad and had never known anything different.

The war held up can developments considerably and very few significant changes occurred during the 1940s. At the end of the decade can manufacturers in Europe began exploring the possibility of using a type of can other than the cone top and McEwan's Export was packaged in a 12 oz flat top in 1948: this is the first re-

corded case of a brewer outside the United States using anything other than a cone top. Indeed, it was still against the trend and when the Hull Brewery, for example, started canning for the first time in 1949, they used cones for their Anchor Export.

The year 1952 saw the general revival of canning for the UK domestic market. British canners were a long way behind their American counterparts: by that year 24% of packaged beer in the United States was being filled in cans.

As the 1950s crept by the cone top gradually became obsolete and was used less and less by

Lees Keglet Bitter and
Robinson's Party Brew
(UK).

above right
**Lederbräu Genuine
Draught Beer was one of
only 26 US brands marketed
in gallons**

the large brewers. The flat top was so much easier to handle, pack and process. The last cones were filled in the late 1950s and it is believed that the last were sold in 1960.

As the flat top began to dominate the market, manufacturers sought ways of improving the quality of their product. Steel had always been used for beer cans, but in 1959 Coors and Gun-

ther experimented with aluminum for the first time. The over-riding advantage of aluminum is that it can be re-cycled and therefore re-used if returned to the canning plant. Both Coors and Gunther produced a 7 oz container, which was an unusually small size. The experiments were a success and during the following decade many brewers were converted away from steel.

**Different methods of
pouring from UK party
cans : Young's Draught
Beer came with two holes
punched in the top, while
Courage Jackpot had a
plastic spout**

opposite
**Two of Britain's earliest
4 pint (2.21 litre) cans,
Blue Can Special Draught
and Truman's Barbecue
Light Bitter, put in
perspective by Lorimer's
Edinburgh Special Ale in a
crimped 440 ml can**

In 1960 an aluminum top was developed for use with a steel can. The disadvantage with the steel top was that it was difficult to punch holes through (at that time this still had to be done to empty the can). It soon became obvious to The Aluminum Company of America that it would be vastly easier to open an aluminum top. Schlitz were among the very first canners to use this type of top.

It is almost certain that the first can with a paper label appeared in 1959 in Hawaii, where Primo Beer was sold in an 11 oz aluminum can. The beer was only marketed for one year and the package became rare for an unusual reason. Each case of 24 cans bore a deposit of 18 cents and so almost all the cans were returned to the

A selection of cans made for British brewers by Metal Box Ltd

brewer; only a few escaped into the hands of beer can collectors. These cans, called 'Shiny Steinies', were withdrawn from production because of problems with the lid and are highly prized today.

As cans became more sophisticated it was clear to brewers and drinkers alike that something would have to be done about the method of opening them. Carrying hole punchers around to pierce the tops was simply not good enough. The first of several possible solutions appeared in 1962, when the Aluminum Company of America invented a tab called a 'lift tab'. When this was pulled off the top it left a hole through which the beer could easily be poured.

The Pittsburgh Brewery were the first to use this type of lift tab and they test marketed their 'new open snap top' in Virginia. Although there were teething troubles in its development, this style of opener caught on and was widely used within three years. It was not until 1967, when the Metal Box Company achieved a breakthrough, that a similar idea was tried in the United Kingdom. It is almost true to say that the British consumers' resistance to canned beer ended with the introduction of what by then became known as the rip top. Once a can could be opened without the use of outside implements it became immediately a vastly more popular item. Within a couple of years rip tops were in production throughout the world.

Meanwhile the United Kingdom was leading the field in a most interesting direction. At some time in the late 1950s—nobody seems quite sure when—the first party can appeared in Britain. It was surprising really that the idea had not been tried before. A large container holding several pints of beer obviously held great attraction for parties where bulk quantities were required. There was no obvious reason why beer should not remain fresh in a large can just as it did in a small one.

A range of can openings — and what they replaced: Pabst's Blue Ribbon 'easy to open' can, with lengthy instructions. The centre can is a collection box — bank cans are made by all the major US brewers

Initially, two sizes of flat top party can were introduced, one holding four pints and one holding seven. Many of the original cans had a hole in the top, sealed by a rubber bung which was removed to pour out the beer. Some had two holes next to each other which made pouring easier. British Oxygen devised a tap which could be used with the can to keep the beer fresh for some days if it was not all drunk at once.

Party cans were an immediate success and many brewers produced that size of can even though they never considered using any other. Flowers, Friary Meux and Charrington were among the first to use the party cans, and Watney's were not far behind.

The Americans were watching and, some years later, National Can developed a US gallon container. The idea never caught on although 26 US party cans were eventually introduced to the market and two others were pre-market tested. Eventually they were all withdrawn.

The main reason for this was that Americans like to drink beer cold, perhaps because the climate is very hot in summer. But to chill a gallon container it had to go into the refrigerator, and when it was in there not much room remained for anything else! The large can was far too unwieldy.

Secondly, the price of the beer was too expensive. The unit cost of beer was higher from a gallon can than any other container and the drinkers did not like that at all. Finally there were problems with the pump device that was developed to go with the cans.

In October 1973 Koch's was the last gallon can to be taken out of production in the United States. Collectors like these big cans very much and many are treasured as momentoes of an interesting experiment in the history of US brewing. Interestingly, a beer called Lederbrau was also issued in a four pint can for the State of Indiana, where the larger size was prohibited. Unlike the United Kingdom where many four pint cans have been issued, this was the only US half gallon and is now keenly prized by collectors.

below
**Truman's Barbecue 5
Draught Bitter 5 pint (2·78
litres) and a supermarket
brand, Co-op Country Pub
5 pint (2·78 litres)**

The gallon cans had a varied reception in Europe. Switzerland has made fairly wide use of them and France and Belgium have each issued one. Sweden toyed with the idea, both Pripps and Tingsryd's producing gallons, but neither had much impact on the Scandinavian market, and both were later dropped. Tingsryd's was in fact filled in the UK by Bass Charrington.

In Germany, however, there are now literally dozens of different beers packaged in this way. In the early 1970s the Germans also started making five litre cans in magnificent barrel shaped containers. These cans, which are very expensive to produce, have proved big sellers in the German domestic market and are much sought after by collectors.

Around 1972 a new and important size variation was introduced in the United Kingdom. The brewers felt that the four pint was just too small for some occasions, so a five pint (or 2·78 l) container was experimented with, being a happy balance between the four and seven pint cans. Issued, as most UK party cans now are, with a flat, sealed top, the five pint can was an

Wadworths Old Timer
4 pint (2·21 litres),
Theakston's Best Bitter
5 pint (2·78 litres) and
Devenish Best Bitter 5 pint
(2·78 litres)

opposite
Crimped cans: McEwan's
Export, with top and
bottom 'knecked in'

opposite
**Pripps' attractive plastic
bottles, introduced in
Sweden early in the 1970s**

**Four distinctive containers:
Switzerland's Uster Brau
with a paper label,
Worthington's plastic
'Dumpy' (UK) a 'merolite'
plastic tube from ICI and
Hamm's popular barrel
shaped can (US)**

ICI's 'merolite' packaging,
for beer and other fizzy
drinks. The flat pouch is
inflated with carbon
dioxide, then filled and
labelled

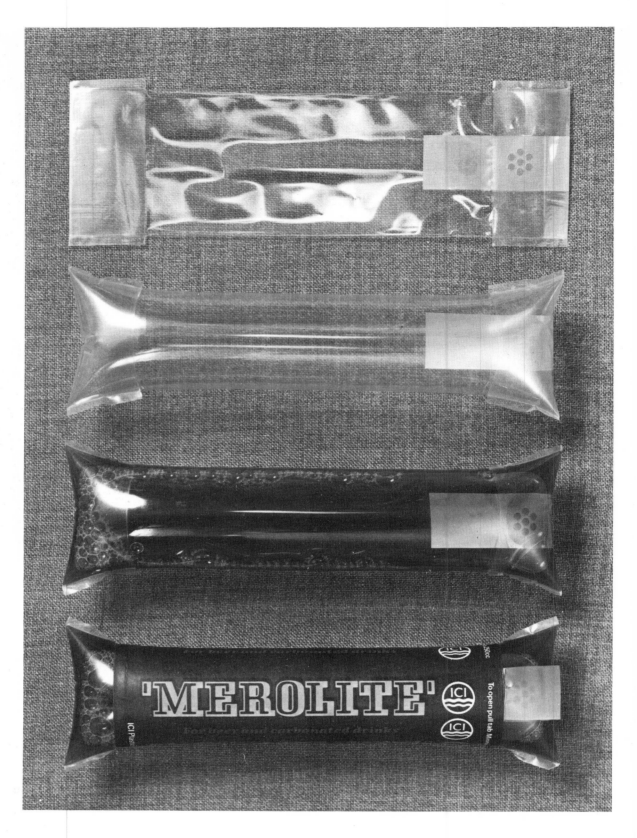

immediate success. Ind Coope Caskette Bitter and Truman Barbecue Five were the first experiments in this size and since then very many others have followed.

Over the last decade, manufacturers have returned to the problem of opening their cans. The big disadvantage with the rip top that came right off the can was that the tab was sharp—if thrown on to the ground it could cut bare feet quite unpleasantly. The State of Oregon banned the use of the rip top completely, and it is quite possible that in time others will follow this lead.

The most popular alternatives devised so far do not involve pulling anything entirely away from the body of the can.

One idea was the 'push top'. This has two buttons on top of the can, one large and one small. Both are pressed inside the can but remain attached to the top. The beer is then poured out through the larger of the two holes. Coors and Anheuser-Busch have both experimented with this type of opening, which was named 'button down' by CanCo, who devised it.

Continental's 'envir-o-can' has a laminated

foil strip attached to the top which is pulled up to reveal holes that have been pre-punched in the top. Once again, the foil remains attached to the can. Coors have tried out an opening which is pushed inwards and which lies against the side of the can. In the meantime the rip top continues to be the most widely used in the United States and around the world.

The latest attempts to produce a two-piece can came in the early 1970s, with the 'drawn and ironed' system. These 'drawn and ironed' cans are made from a flat sheet of aluminum from which a disc is blanked out and formed into a cup. This cup is ironed into a seamless body with very thin walls but a thicker bottom. The body becomes more rigid when filled, due to the pressure of the beer inside.

The advantage of this type of container is that the absence of a side and bottom seam means that the container has two fewer places where it could leak. The absence of a side seam means also that the package may be decorated all the way round – an advantage to the breweries' advertising departments.

Following the success of experiments in the United States, drawn and ironed cans were tried out in the United Kingdom by Metal Box in 1972. It is estimated that by the end of the 1970s half the market will be taken up by drawn and ironed cans. Both tinplate and aluminum can be used for these containers and some people feel, surprisingly enough, that tinplate is leading the way.

The big development of the mid-1970s has been the 'crimped' or 'knecked in' can. This involves a reduction in the diameter of the top and bottom of the can, making space saving possible which in turn makes multiple packaging much easier. There is a steady movement towards crimped cans both in the United States and in Britain, where Bass Charrington, Hall & Woodhouse and Thwaites have already converted their entire canning plant to fill this type of can. Usually, when a crimped can is issued, its design is exactly the same as that used before; the only difference that may be detected is that the can is no longer straight all the way down the side.

Recently there have been attempts to introduce a plastic container for beer. In Sweden, so-called 'plastic bottles' were introduced at the start of the decade. These are now widely on sale and are the most successful example of the use of plastic for beer packaging. In the middle of 1975 plastic beer cans were tried in England by Bass Charrington. They were called Dumpies and had a plastic body attached to a normal aluminum rip top. The container, balanced on three squat points and very unattractive, was far from being a success.

There is little likelihood of plastic making immediate inroads into the can manufacturing markets. After the first 40 years of the beer can the industry is alive and doing very well: it seems ready to face whatever innovations the future may produce.

Stages in the 'drawn and ironed' process for aluminium cans with no side seam: the cup is drawn, redrawn, ironed, ironed again and then trimmed to produce a flange for the top to fit on

Collector's items

Like anything else, a can is worth whatever the market will stand. The old forces of supply and demand are the ultimate determinants of exchange value. Most of the buying and selling of cans goes on in America, although the world's largest dealer is based in England. So market factors in the States decide what can values shall be and it is not necessarily those cans which are hardest to find that obtain top market prices.

Up to a point, collectors follow fashion and several times in this decade a collector or a few collectors have created popularity for one particular can. This has resulted in sharply rising prices. The can itself may not necessarily be rare: fashion has chased up the price. Perhaps the very best example of this occurred in the case of Tennent's Temporary Can, produced in

Scotland by Tennent's of Glasgow in a 333 ml container. The can has an interesting story.

In the late fall of 1974 there was a chronic shortage of tin plate in Britain following the three day working week of the winter before. Tennent's could not get enough tinplate to make their usual 440 ml steel can for the busy Christmas season, so they arranged to be supplied with around a million aluminum cans. Instead of the smiling faces of the eight girls who normally adorn their lager cans in the British domestic market, these cans bore only the legend that this was the usual Tennent's Lager in a temporary can.

The container was only on sale for some six weeks and during that time very few crossed the Atlantic. For a while there was no spectacular demand, but then a St Louis collector

opposite
Playmate Malt Liquor ran foul of American copyright laws

far left
Tennent's Temporary Can, on sale for just six weeks in late 1974.

Amana Beer (US), the most wanted can of 1976

featured the can in a nationwide beer can magazine. Overnight a terrific demand blew up, as people heard about this rare can that had come and gone. Within 12 months specimens were changing hands at prices as high as $100.

This is an example of sheep following sheep. Because everybody wanted the same can at the same time, demand and a market short of stock pushed the price sky high. The can *is* rare and there *are* only about 200 in collections around the world, but nevertheless its true market value is nearer the $20 mark.

The same thing happened with James Bond 007: historically perhaps the world's most wanted set of cans. Shortly after the James Bond cult became fashionable internationally in the early 1960s, the National Brewing Company in Phoenix, Arizona, had the brilliant idea of producing beer in a package styled after Bond. They made a brew that was a mixture of premium beer and malt liquor and packaged it in a set of seven cans bearing pictures of four different girls, posed against the background of different London scenes.

It seemed the idea could hardly fail, but it did –with a bang that would have alarmed Bond himself! The beer flopped in the test market and within six months both the brew and the packaging were withdrawn. Within a few weeks of their issue the cans were obsolete. During that time very few sets had reached the collectors, but an enterprising businessman bought the remaining stocks from the brewers and began releasing them on to the market one set at a time. The demand was so great that by the middle 1970s prices of around $2,000 were being paid for a complete set.

Containers depicting girls have always been popular and a pair of cans dating from the early 1960s command big prices. They are Playmate Malt Liquor and Playmate Premium Beer, produced by the Sunshine Brewing Company of Reading, Pennsylvania, which bore pictures of a most desirable, and very female, playmate. Unfortunately the Playboy organization considered that the whole thing was an infringement of their copyright of the name 'Playmate' and succeeded in getting the designs withdrawn from the market. The cans are scarce and much wanted: prices for the pair are rising well above $300.

The most expensive new issue of 1976 was Amana Beer, sold in a US 12 oz can in January 1976 by the Cold Spring Brewing Company, Cold Spring, Minnesota. After the beer had been on sale for a few days, Amana Colonies took out an injunction to prevent the use of their name. The beer had no sooner appeared on the market than it was gone for good.

Before it had been removed some fast operators moved in and bought all the stock that they could lay their hands on. Then, having emptied them, they began releasing the cans to the market at prices ranging from $5 to $25 each. So many cans were scooped up in this way (the number has been estimated at 40,000) that they could not be considered scarce by any stretch of the imagination. A vast wave of publicity surrounding the incident led many collectors to pay absurd prices to obtain specimens of this can.

Few cans outside the United States have commanded high prices, which is mainly because of low demand. American collectors are chiefly interested in cans from their own country, although specialist collectors spend

far right
Soul Stout (US), offended the National Association for the Advancement of Colored Peoples

Marks and Spencer Special Country Bitter, sold in a 2·21 litre party can with a paper label (UK). It was only available for two short test marketings.

much time and effort searching for older and rarer cans from any source. Early cone tops in mint condition are always highly prized. For example, Coronation Brew (marketed in 1937 by Simonds Brewery at Reading, England, to mark the coronation of King George VI) could be considered almost priceless. The only specimen known to exist in a collection is held by Bill Christensen of Madison, New Jersey.

Soul Mellow Yellow Beer and Soul Stout Malt Liquor join James Bond 007 as the world's most wanted cans: like 007, the demand has pushed the market price way above $225 a can. Mellow Yellow was made in 12 and 16 oz packages, while Malt Liquor was issued only in 16 oz, although a 12 oz size was being prepared at the time of its demise. Both beers were brewed by the Maier Brewing Corporation in Los Angeles, with the black population especially in mind–hence the name 'Soul'. Contrary to popular belief, the beers were first marketed in 1967, and about one million cans were made in all. But Maier had not anticipated an objection from the National Association for the Advancement of Colored People to the name of 'Soul'. Their protest was so strong that the brands were withdrawn after two years on the market.

For some unknown reason, the brew and the background caught collectors' imaginations and prices reached extraordinary heights. The cans are scarce but not rare and one can only conclude that there is no sense in some col-

The so-called 'Porno' cans, issued by Denmark's Irma supermarket chain in December 1974

right
The celebrated Miss
Rheingold series (US).

opposite top left
Storzette calorie-
controlled beer (US) –
decorated with an orchid
to appeal to women

opposite top right
Finlandia Gold in a rare
Finnish can sold by a
German super market

opposite bottom
Christmas cans from
Sweden and (centre) Iron
City (US)

below
The celebrated James Bond
007 series (US)

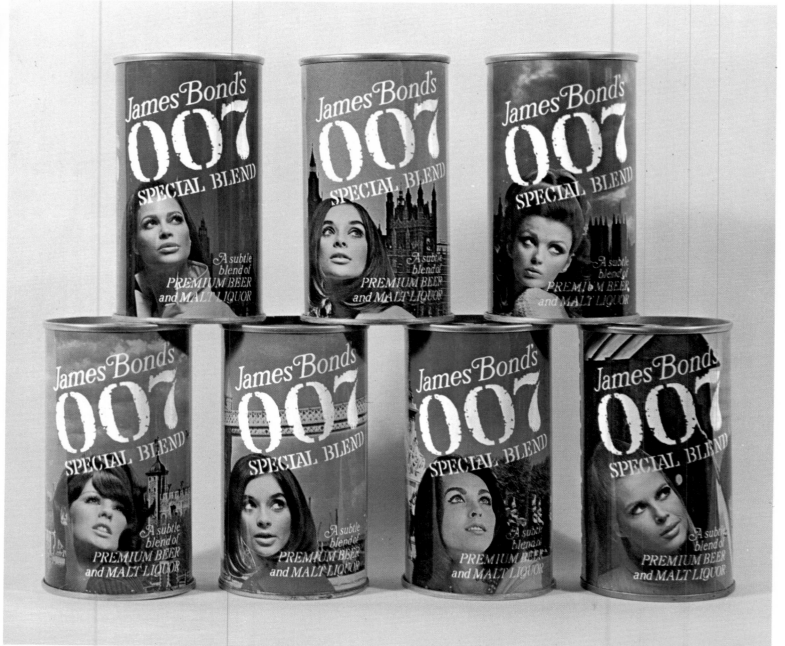

46

lectors' ideas of comparative prices – Astro Malt Liquor and Value Line Stout Malt Liquor, for example, are much scarcer than Soul but nowhere near so highly priced.

The most sought after cans of 1975 were without doubt the so called 'Porno' cans. Granges Brewery of Grangesbergs, Sweden, fill Lysl and Fadl cans for the Danish supermarket chain Irma. Lysl, a very low alcohol beer, was packaged in four different cans bearing poems and line drawings of nudes. When the second series came to be issued in December 1974, a story was written and sent around the world claiming that 'pornographic beer' was being produced. Huge quantities were sold in Copenhagen alone.

The demand from collectors for these Porno cans was intense, although most collectors must have been disappointed when they saw the actual product, which though unusual was hardly erotic. Now these cans, which have been

superseded by a set of four bearing colored wavy lines, are prized curios rather than essentially valuable and have a market value of maybe $4 per can.

Cans with paper labels are rarely issued and collectors regard them highly. They are invariably produced by smaller brewers who buy quantities of standard or 'universal' containers from the can manufacturers and paste on their own label. This is cheaper than having a can produced with one's own design. Uster Brau from Switzerland in a 350 ml can is a prized example, while some of the few put out by tiny German brewers are extremely rare.

Perhaps the scarcest of all is an English party can put out by the famous English supermarket chain Marks and Spencer in the winter of 1975. It was a 2·21 litre can and was on sale initially for only two months, although it re-appeared some nine months later – it has now finally been withdrawn. Filled with Ruddle's County Ale, its label bore a picture of an old world corn-harvesting scene. The can is difficult to track down and probably only a dozen specimens exist in collections. Each has a market value of around $40.

Little known, and certainly not in demand, one of the world's rarest sets is that of five cans put out by Eldridge Pope Ltd from their Dorchester Brewery in 1973. The set consisted of Dorset Brown Ale, Crystal Light Ale and Green Top Ale in three cans bearing different colored pictures of a Dorset huntsman, together with Konig Lager and Konig Diabetic Lager in plain cans. These were not issued to the public.

The brewers had so much trouble with the canning line, which they had bought second-hand, that they scrapped the idea of canning and dumped the cans. So this set has the unique distinction of existing but never being retailed. A very few sets reached the United States and they are irreplaceable: much rarer than 007, but simply unrecognized by most collectors.

A very unusual series was issued in Orange, New Jersey, and Brooklyn, New York, in the autumn of 1956, when the Liebmann Breweries produced Miss Rheingold Extra Dry Lager. This beer appeared in six different containers sold in sets, and each one bore a different picture of a Miss Rheingold. Consumers were asked to say which of the girls pictured on the sides of the cans they liked best. The winning girl was Margie McNally and the can bearing her picture was actually re-issued with the title 'Miss Rheingold 1957'. A mint set of these cans would be worth a fortune today.

For major collectors, like Ron Moermond of Denver, Colorado, European party cans have immense importance, particularly those that are harder to track down. An excellent example is Stella Artois 1366: one of only two Dutch five litre cans. It is filled at the Valkenswaard brewery of the Belgium-based company. Recent German issues of these barrel-shaped cans, like Moninger Pils and Saarfurt Pils, are equally keenly sought.

Quite a number of specialist American collectors are very enthusiastic about Bock cans, which have an unusual and interesting story. Bock beer is a special brew produced in the United States each spring; it is not made at any other time. In taste it is roughly similar to English brown ale. 'Bock' is the German word for 'goat' and all Bock cans bear a picture of a goat's head. Some of the early Bock beer cans were very handsome, with massive goat's heads. Almost all have been US 12 oz size, so one of the world's rarest cans is Schmidt's Old Style Bock Beer which is the only Bock quart yet discovered. This can was marketed just before the Second World War.

Some containers are noteworthy because their contents were brewed for a particular

below and opposite
These pictures of regimental pipers were a great success for Tennent's in Scotland and around the world.

market. Quite a number of brewers in Britain make sugar-free beer for diabetics. To date only one such brand has ever been canned and that was Eldridge Pope's Konig Diabetic Lager— one of the ill-fated set of five cans that never appeared on the market. Carlton Dietale is a well known Australian brand for diabetics, while the American Storzette beer was calorie-controlled, and produced specially for women. It was packaged in an appropriately modest 8 oz container with an orchid on the side, to appeal to female drinkers.

One of the most famous and valued American sets is the Gretz Fleet Car series, produced in the mid-1950s by the Gretz Brewing Company. This set, which now looks very dated, features a dozen different sports cars that were popular at the time. Strangely enough, they include only two American-made cars! Very few complete sets exist today and a set in mint condition would certainly command a price of around $600. It is rather surprising that more containers have not been issued featuring cars: the masculine relationship between beer and automobiles seems so obvious.

Gretz gave much serious consideration to marketing in the 1950s. Their Tooner Schooner Beer appeared in 1955 and was represented by 19 different cans in all. Six different cans were each issued in three different colors and there was also a single candy-striped can. They were called 'Tooner' Schooner because they bore the words of popular songs on the side. Doubtless the words and the contents mixed well at drinking parties!

One of the most unusual series ever produced came out in the United States in the 1950s (the classic period for US sets) when Drewry's of South Bend, Indiana, issued a set of six cans depicting horoscopes. They also issued a set showing people how to read their characters, and another series from the same brewer depicted six different sporting activities.

Little attention has been paid to humor on beer cans, although some comic cans have been produced. Lucky Brewing of San Francisco issued the biggest spoof of all in the shape of King Snedley, a magnificent example of original packaging. This beer, designed to appeal to teenagers and those in their early twenties, carried the motif 'beer with us' and pictures of King Snedley, Princess Fatoona and others. The can was taken off the market and achieved quite a scarcity value, but to the delight of most enthusiasts it re-appeared recently bearing the boast that 'this terrific can contains 12 fluid oz of King Snedley's swell beer'.

Rather unusual and very little known are Jul 01 cans. 'Jul' is Swedish for 'Christmas' and Jul 01 (Christmas Beer) is issued at the festive season by a small number of regional brewers in Sweden. One American brewer also follows this idea: Iron City issue very pleasant and decorative containers for Christmas.

The American legend of Paul Bunyan is brought to life on a can of that name. It commemorates the North American wood chopper who, so the story goes, cut down a whole forest with a single stroke. The can shows Bunyan, axe and all, in a pleasant reminder that fiction as well as fact has its place in modern packaging.

Finally there is the curious story of French '76 Sparkling Malt Liquor, another US can, which was issued by the National Brewing Company from their Baltimore brewery and failed to sell. After some thought National re-issued the brew in a different package labelled Colt 45 and it was an immediate success. This is an unusual example of a beer recovering lost market ground just by a change of name. Colt 45 is now well known in several countries, and is 'one of the very few beers' sold in Britain which is packaged only in cans.

Cans for the occasion

Beer cans are often issued to mark occasions and events, just like stamps and medallions. A good example is Charter Ale, which was brewed and canned by Phipps' Brewery at Northampton, England, for the Lacon Brewery at Norwich in 1958. This 10 oz flat top was made to commemorate the 750th anniversary of the granting of a Royal Charter to Great Yarmouth and it bears the falcon crest which was the sign of the Lacon Brewery and the crest of the Lacon family. This can is only known to exist in one collection and is quite valuable.

The United States Bi-Centennial year of 1976 saw a great number of instant commemorative cans. Ortlieb's Collectors Series and Schmidt's 'The Beer For The Bi-Centennial' are just two examples of dozens that flooded the market. Others include Iron City and Falstaff, whose can bears a personal message from the chairman of the board. None have more than sentimental value at present, though they will doubtless command a small premium in years to come.

BCCA have created their own commemoratives by issuing a special can to each member attending the canventions. Most valuable of these is the Busch Bavarian Beer collector's edition, issued for the first ever convention (subsequently known as canvention). This is the ordinary Busch can overprinted specially for BCCA.

In 1973 BCCA used a Schlitz can which gave full details on the back of the third canvention, held that year at Cincinnati. Some Chapters have even issued their own souvenir cans. These have curiosity value but little else. The Hawkeye Chapter, for example, issued a can to mark their hosting of the fifth canvention, held in Des Moines, Iowa, in 1975.

World Wide Beer Can Collectors have issued special cans to mark the occasion of their annual shows. Their 1976 can was particularly noteworthy: its decoration followed the Bi-Centennial theme. Once again, many of these cans exist and their value is minimal.

Special issue cans often disappear from the market before being noticed by collectors, and this may make them particularly valuable. One of the very least known special issues, and one of the most exciting, is Castrol New Formula GTX 2 which was issued in 1975 for use at an oil

exhibition. This can was filled at Ottakringer Brewery in Vienna and is an exact replica of the GTX 2 oil can. Only some 50 specimens exist in collections.

Another can put out for promotional use was United Airlines Brew 747 which was issued in 1973 purely as a gimmick. The can never contained beer but had different souvenirs inside each of the six cans. Two years later, Expo '75 was marked by the issue of a Japanese can from Orion Breweries, illustrated with color pictures of the exhibits.

A quite extraordinary can was issued by Tennent's around 1970 as a promotional gimmick. The can exhorted consumers to buy six

The Busch Bavarian can bears the label produced for BCCA's first convention, held in Missouri in 1971

BCCA cans for 1975 and 1976

In 1975 BCCA's Hawkeye Chapter hosted the 5th National convention in Iowa, and issued their own commemorative can

of the cans: if they did so they could win £1.00. Nobody knows how much this cost Tennent's!

Courage (Australia) are one of the world's newest brewers and they have devoted much time to devising unusual containers which will attract the public to their products. Best known in collections is America's Cup 1974, the special container issued to mark the yacht race held that year. Courage Draught was the only Australian beer chosen for use by the crew of the Australian yacht.

Sporting themes have been used a great deal in Australia. Courage have issued cans with Test Match statistics to mark games of cricket against England. Toohey's have also celebrated test matches and have issued a can with a photograph of a match in progress. In 1976 West End issued a container to commemorate Delvin Dancer, who 10 years before won more consecutive races than any other racehorse in Australian history. Courage have also issued cans honoring Australian football stars.

Certainly one of the most impressive new issues of 1976 was Hudepohl Pure Grain Beer issued by the Hudepohl Brewing Company, Cincinnati, to congratulate the Cincinnati Reds on their victory in the US football 'world' championships.

The Karlsberg Brewery in Hamburg, Germany, issued a most attractive 12 oz can some years ago featuring a colorful photograph of their brewery taken from the air. Only one example is known to exist and the brewers

Hudepohl Pure Grain Beer congratulates the Cincinnati Reds on winning the US football championship

West End celebrate two Australian horse races: Inter-Dominion Trotting and the Great Eastern Steeplechase

53

themselves have forgotten for what purpose the can was issued in the first place!

Another special can came out of Germany in 1975, to commemorate a paint exhibition: it was issued by the Inmont paint manufacturers. A similar can was used in the United Kingdom in 1974 when a 275 ml Long Life can was superimposed with advertising material for Pinchin Johnson, again for use at a paint exhibition.

The most highly priced commemorative cans in history are three whose values have been driven up by the publicity that they have received in collectors' magazines: they all come from New Zealand. One of them, Bavarian Old Style Beer, was brewed by New Zealand Brew-

eries for Operation Deep Freeze—a scientific program at the South Pole.

New Zealand Breweries also issued Deep Cove and West Arm beer, to mark the construction of a giant hydro-electric project. Work commenced in 1963 and was completed in 1973. During that time a camp was established at Deep Cove at the top of a fjord on the west coast, and an original brew of beer, in a specially created container, was supplied to the workers there from August 1967 to November 1968. These immensely rare cans reached few collectors and command prices over $100 each. West Arm, made for workers on the other side of the fjord in 1968 is equally scarce.

A most interesting item is the Original Oyster House Beer brewed in a 12 oz can and issued by The Pittsburgh Brewing Company. This container features the famous original Oyster House Tavern, which is located in Market Square and has been a favorite with the citizens of Pittsburgh since 1870. It has been designated a historical landmark of the city. The can features black and white photographs of the inside of the tavern.

One of England's most famous beers, Greene King's Abbot Ale, is marketed in a fine 275 ml can showing the noted Abbot who made it

famous; and an old English office, the Peculier of Masham, is remembered on a can put out by Theakston under the name Old Peculier.

A very valuable can was issued in 1969 by the Felinfoel Brewery at Llanelli, Wales. Prince's Ale, in a 275 ml can, designed to commemorate the Investiture of HRH Prince Charles as Prince of Wales, is little known and only around two dozen exist in collections. The can bears the royal crest and the Welsh arms and is worth about $30. Any container bearing a design connected with the English Royal Family commands an instant premium.

New Zealand Breweries produced special cans for a hydroelectricity project at Deep Cove and a scientific expedition to the South Pole: Operation Deep Freeze

opposite
Germany's Rewe supermarket chain issued a set of soccer cans for the 1970 World Cup in Mexico

International cans

Let us make a tour of the world, visiting those countries which are involved substantially in beer canning. We shall start our journey in the United States, although it is sad to say that the country which spawned the beer can is now the one which produces the dullest and most uninteresting containers of almost anywhere. Most of the US cans are 12 oz and most are unimaginative.

The Pittsburgh Brewing Company have been one of the very few US brewers over the last few years to produce a range of interesting containers. They have issued special cans celebrating Christmas, a series with sketches of local landmarks, many different sporting scenes honoring local football teams and stars, and a host of others.

Without doubt, Pittsburgh's most famous and popular can is Olde Frothingslosh, which makes famous an extremely large woman rejoicing in the name of 'Miss Olde Frothingslosh 1969'. This can originated from a joke on local radio KDKA on which a disc jockey used to give commercials for an imaginary beer – Olde Frothingslosh. In 1968, the Pittsburgh Brewery responded to the joke and issued a beer can with that name. It was not on sale long at first, but it came back to the market in 1973 and since then has appeared in a long succession of different colored cans.

This clever piece of marketing features a girl from a 'small town outside Pittsburgh which is considerably smaller since she left'. Her occupation is given as a trapeze artist and supposedly she is educating herself by studying arc welding at night. Her hobbies, the can states, include soap carving and ballet. Finally, the message concludes that her formula for success is 'Think Big'!

Hamm's of St Paul, Minnesota, have been both adventurous and original in using a 12 oz can made in the shape of a beer barrel. Acme Beer from the Acme Brewing Company in San Francisco won the award as BCCA Can of The Year in 1975. Their can featured scenes of merriment and written information about The Acme Brewing process. Another Can of The Year (winner in 1973) was Our Beer in a colorful can depicting a barrel and a glass. It was brewed and filled by Jos Huber Brewing from Monroe, Wisconsin.

Schmidt of St Paul, Minnesota, is one of the few US brewers currently producing sets. Schmidt produced its first series of containers depicting wildlife and nature scenes in 1950, and they have been popular ever since. Since that time more than 20 different pictures have been issued, including outdoor sporting scenes. The pictures look rather old fashioned, but remain attractive.

Crossing the Atlantic we arrive in England, which is one of the world's major canning

opposite
BCCA's 'Can of the Year' winners: Our Beer (1973) and Acme (1975)

Five cans from Schmidt's outdoor series

countries with well over 250 different cans in production. All the major national brewers can in large quantities, as do many of the numerous regional brewers. More and more brands from more and more brewers appear all the time, many of them with very pleasing decoration.

Containers are produced in 275 ml (9 oz) and 440 ml (16 oz) sizes for the home market; some are produced in 330 ml or 340 ml (12 oz) for sale to ships' stores and for export. Those made for the merchant navy are often still fitted with steel tops to prevent naked feet running on decks being cut by the rip top cans. Most of the major supermarket chains have beer canned for them under their own brand names, and shandy cans are also produced in large quantities. A mixture of lemonade or ginger beer and beer, shandy is a popular light drink in Britain.

Many of the early English canners were taken

over during the 1960s and have disappeared without trace. The name of Simonds, which was taken into what is now the Courage Group 15 years ago, survives on cans only in Malta. Barclay's, another company taken into the Courage Group, lives on through Barclay's Sparkling Beer, which is still made for export.

The Hull Brewery, later the North Country Brewery, ceased canning in 1975, but not before it had produced a whole stream of beautiful cans, the early examples of which showed sailing ships. Later they were noted for their Black Beauty Stout and Golden Export 275 ml cans. Another North of England independent, Greenall Whitley, produced a trio of excellent cans—Grunhalle Lager, Family Light (withdrawn in 1975) and Champion Pale Ale.

The largest contract canners in the West of England, Hall and Woodhouse, have for years been famous for their Badger Beers, which are always marketed in attractive cans. Most sought after are the old 340 ml cans produced for export. Three of these bore the badger theme and the fourth pictured the Norman keep at Corfe Castle which was destroyed by Cromwell's army in 1646. Hall and Woodhouse also canned West Side Lager for A. H. Rackham Ltd; this little known can bore a picture of an alpine scene and was withdrawn in December 1975.

Much thought has gone into the design of English party cans, many of which are quite impressive. Among the best examples are Huntsman Homecan, which pictures Eldridge Pope's famous Wessex huntsman in his red coat, and Boddington's Bodcan with the brewer's bee theme. Ruddle's County, Ruddle's Traditional, David Greig Traditional and Key Traditional have all carried in a differently colored can the same picture of a real English outdoor feast.

King Snedley, from San Francisco's Lucky Brewing Co.

Three of a set of game birds by Schmidt's

Marks and Spencer's Pale Ale, Special Bitter and Export Pale

Supermarket cans by
Giant Food (US), Grand
Union (US) and Marks and
Spencer (UK)

opposite
Olde Frothingslosh: a bevy
of different coloured cans
featuring the mighty lady

Ben Truman Export and Co-Op Country Pub were both illustrated with pictures of English pub scenes.

Since 1958 Tennent's of Scotland have produced series after series of cans illustrated with pin-ups. Tennent's Sweet Stout still appears in Scotland in 16 oz cans, with 12 different pictures of 'Ann' in various poses, as does Younger's Sweetheart Stout showing a very old-fashioned looking girl. Tennent's Lager Lovlies have been much sought after recently. In the very early days Tennent's Lager showed pictures of the Scottish countryside.

We noted that British canning began in Wales at the Felinfoel Brewery. This still exists and produces two 275 ml cans Double Dragon and Double Strong in containers made colorful by the Welsh Dragon theme. Canning is almost non-existent in Ireland, except that Harp and Guinness are brewed there and Monk Export is imported direct from Scotland. There is a

above left
Sun Charm Shandy and Lime and Lager

above
Brock Gold Medal Lager, with a view of Corfe Castle, and Hull Brewery's Golden Export, with a hunting scene (UK)

opposite
Five British supermarket cans

left
Another UK 4 pint (2·21 litre) can

below left
Abbot Ale and Theakston's Old Peculier (UK)

below
Double Strong Ale and Double Dragon, from the Felinfoel Brewery

Ten of the girls who have decorated Tennent's Lager

opposite
Six German 5 litre cans made for use with 'Fass Frisch' dispensers

More from the Tennent's range: a series of Scots views

opposite
Tennent's Sweet Stout: devoted to Ann

below left
Three European cans: Bofferding (Luxembourg), Da Gama (Portugal) and Lamot (Belgium)

below
Laurentide (France), Younger's Monk Export (Scotland), Castlemaine XXXX (Australia), Dreher Forte (Italy), and a promotion can for Wiederhold, a German company producing printer's inks

growing trend to brew overseas beers under licence in Britain and to market them in British cans: Kronenbourg, Tuborg, Carlsberg and Holsten Pilsner are examples.

Across the channel, France produces a few cans – 33 Export, Mutzig and Kronenbourg are the best known. The most interesting can, however, is Pelforth's superb 3·86 litre container which bears a reproduction of Pieter Breughel's famous painting *Wedding Dance in the Open Air*. This most keenly prized 'gallon' can has appeared in two versions: the first, and scarcer, was identified by a paper label. Pelforth also fill a 340 ml can.

It is very difficult to find canned beer in Belgium, although Stella Artois is filled in a 340 ml can and Lamot appears in a splendid container of the same size, which is illustrated with pictures of lovers. Wiels also fill a 3·86 litre can from their Brussels brewery, with a party

Denner de Luxe (Switzerland), Eku Pils (Germany), Haldengut (Switzerland), Alpirsbacher Pilsner (Germany) and Royal beer from the Munich Hofbräuhaus

scene on the side.

Holland, like Belgium, is a country where canned beer is rarely found in the shops, although there is a great deal of canning done by the Skol Brewery–mainly for export. Exotic brands such as Jaeger Beer, Red Point Spezial and Oranjeboom Dark Lager are made for consumption outside the country. Bavaria Bier was once filled in Holland in 3·86 litre cans: the only Dutch 'gallon' to date.

Like the United States and Britain, Germany is a giant producer of canned beer, almost all in the 12 oz size. Until 1976 each can was 350 ml but in that year all the brewers began switching to the slightly smaller 333 ml size due to a change in the type of machinery used in filling. Most of the cans are fairly ordinary, although some like Eku Pils and Moninger Export bear impressive artwork.

Germany is chiefly noted for its remarkable

quantity of party cans in both 3·86 litre and 5·0 litre sizes. Most of these big cans are made under licence for Fass Frisch ('barrel fresh') and are specifically designed for use with a beer dispensing pump designed by that company. It is impossible to estimate how many different 3·86 litre cans have been marketed, but certainly over 50. In 1975 it was known that there were 65 different 5·0 litre cans in production and the number is likely to grow. These are among the world's most impressive cans.

Italy has only one brewery which produces cans of distinction, although quite a number of different brewers fill cans. Dreher SPA brewery in Pedavena has produced many different cans in numerous sets, all showing sports scenes. These cans are hard to find and are much sought after. The cans put out by the other brewers tend to be uninteresting; they are all 340 ml size and many are made from aluminum, which

Stella Artois (Belgium) and Erzquell Pils (Germany) are both sold in 5 litre cans; like Lamot (Belgium), Stella is also sold in a 350 ml can

does not lend itself to good artwork.

Few countries export as many beers as Switzerland. Cardinal was one of the first to be sold in the United States, where it is still found, along with Hurlimann Spezial and some others, all produced in 350 ml cans. Other well known names are Schutzengarten, Lowenbrau Zurich and Haldengut.

Austria has several famous brewers whose wares are exported all over the world. Gold Fassl, Steffl Export and Golden Rock are all well known beers and all are available in cans, but none of their designs justify special note. If we travel north to Scandinavia, however, we find another story.

Environmental legislation limits the number of beer cans produced in Denmark, so most of the beer brewed there is filled in bottles or sold in kegs. Carlsberg, whose cans are normally rather uninteresting, produce an excellent 355 ml container for exporting their Elephant

opposite and below
Two sets by Granges of Sweden: Brygghusöl and Fatöl

left
Tingsryd's Skeppar: a set of seven

73

74

opposite
**Four examples from Birka
Beer's set of 25 cans**

**Schneider (Argentina),
Pelforth's (France), Aguila
Imperial (Spain), Pokal
(Sweden), Hansa (South
West Africa) and Zulia
(Venezuela)—an inter-
national selection**

Mediterranean cans: Keo (Cyprus) and Fix (Greece)

Israel's OK Pilsner

Beer, which is mainly sold on board Danish ships. The Albani Brewery market the most unusual and exciting Danish can, containing their Albani Fad. It is a colorful orange can bearing a cartoon of Vikings drinking beer.

Granges of Grangesbergs in Sweden have produced a whole host of different sets for the Irma supermarket chain in Denmark and these are very highly prized. Their Lysl and Fadl beers are sold in 450 ml cans, usually in sets of four. The various issues have included the famous 'Porno' cans, cartoons of people playing and on the beach, and series of containers just colored with wavy lines. They are hard to obtain and command premium prices.

In Sweden itself, there is an almost unending range of bright, colorful cans and much attention is paid to the quality of the artwork, which is outstanding judged by the most critical beer can collecting standards. Sweden has produced many sets which are very keenly prized. The rarest set of all is Birka Beer, which depicts on the reverse 25 different historical relics and weapons. Very few complete sets exist.

Granges, who fill the Irma cans found in Denmark, also produce Brygghusol, which com-

prises a set of five cans each showing people at work. They are most famous, however, for their set of 25 containers each bearing magnificent photographs of a different Swedish province. Their finest set is for their Export Beer, which is marketed in sets of eight, each showing a master painting. The brewery's most recent issue, Flaggol, is another excellent and original can decorated with the English royal standard.

Pripps Fatol is very well known and is packaged in a set of three different cans showing warships at sea. This nautical theme was seen also on Tingsryd's obsolete set of seven cans, showing line drawings of various ships. Sailor Export and Pripps Bla Mellanol are more recent examples of other containers showing ships. The influence of the North Sea has been seen a lot on Scandinavian cans.

Many other brewers issue packages showing drinking scenes. Till Fatol with two men raising glasses, Pokal Mellanol depicting a full glass of beer, Faxe Fad with a scene in a bar, and Abro Fatol depicting a tankard are all good examples. Lappland issues at least two cans, both illustrating the beautiful countryside in the area of the Arctic Circle. It may be argued that

77

above
KB (Australia) and Brador (Canada)

above right
Taiwan Beer, and Holsten Pilsner exported to Hong Kong

opposite
Polar (Venezuela), Brahma Chopp and Brahma Extra (Brazil) and Moctezuma Brewery's XXX (Mexico)

Five birds from Suntory of Japan

Suntory golf cans: the design changed when Suntory adopted aluminum (below)

for excellence of packaging, the brewers of Sweden are way ahead of every other country.

Norway has about a dozen canned beers on sale, and almost every Norwegian brewer produces identical designs with different coloring for each of two brands, Pils and Export. Dahls Pils/Export, Tou Pils/Export are typical examples, although the Tou cans are particularly attractive. They have the same drinking scene, but with a slight color difference.

Finland produces only 450 ml containers and they are little known to collectors, although Finlandia Blue and Finlandia Gold beers have been sold in other countries, including the United States. Apart from these Aura and Karjala are perhaps the best known. None have remarkable designs.

Cyprus boasts only one canned beer, but the package is a cracker–one of the world's most beautiful cans. Produced in both 340 ml and 440 ml by Keo Ltd, Keo Beer is a pilsener made from the finest malt and choicest hops. Its sleek yellow container has classical lines with simple black and white wording and a gold crest superimposed.

Malta, like Cyprus, has only one brewery large enough to fill cans. Over the years, Simonds, Farsons, Cisk (which has close connections with the Courage Group in England) has marketed its lager and pale ale in a mixture of 275, 340 and 440 ml cans; only the 340 ml size is currently used.

South and West Africa have a flourishing brewing industry which uses 340 ml and 450 ml cans. Among their more interesting products are Hansa Pilsener, which carries a map of West Africa; Rogue, which depicts a rogue elephant; and Madison–the only beer in the world to honor an American president. European beer is sold in African cans: the English Whitbread Gold Crest, the German Kronenbrau 1308 and the Dutch Amstel Lager can all be found. Even American influence is felt through Carling Beer, which is packaged in both sizes of cans. East Africa, meanwhile, is the home of one of the world's least known cans–MacMahon Special, made in Lourenço Marques, Mozambique. It is filled in a 340 ml can.

Malaysia is famed the world over for Tiger Beer, which sailors from Singapore take with them wherever they go. The container has been exported all over the world and is found in many collections. So also is Anchor Beer, which hails from the Middle East.

Japanese cans are in huge demand. Several brewers, most notably Suntory, have produced remarkable containers. The Suntory cans include series of golf scenes, football matches, railway scenes and, perhaps most famous of all, birds. The Suntory bird cans may be the prettiest cans ever made. They were made only for the home market until very recently, when a few were exported to the US.

Sapporo is another Japanese brewer to make cans with sporting themes. Among others, they have marketed containers showing athletes in action. It is a pity that the main range of Japanese cans produced for export have been unremarkable aluminum containers.

Australia and New Zealand are both noted for their beer drinkers, who are catered for with a wide range of cans. Apart from commemorative cans, however, neither country has produced any noteworthy designs–Cooper's Big Barrel, showing a drinking scene, is one of the better examples.

Big Barrel Lager from Cooper's (Australia) and New Zealand's Leopard Strong Beer

Building a collection

It is probably easier to start collecting beer cans than almost anything else. In fact, the only big problem facing the would-be enthusiast is where to put the cans. This is a serious difficulty, so before starting to collect beer cans a conscious decision should be made on where to display them. Generally speaking a whole room, or the walls of a whole room, needs to be allotted to the enterprise.

One reason why there are so many collectors in the United States and so few elsewhere is that many Americans have basements in their houses, which can be used for recreation. Such a room can readily be used to house a large collection. Most Europeans simply do not have that amount of spare space and cannot decide where to display a thousand and more cans. For it must be admitted that cans do take up a great deal of room.

The best type of room to use is a second living room, study or family room. One that is used for recreation rather than the main sitting room. If this is impossible, a bedroom may be used, but this is less satisfactory. As a last resort, garage space or even the sides of stairways are possible sites.

Once a place has been selected, considerable thought must be given to the method of display, for there is little point in a collection that cannot be inspected easily. Unless the cans are displayed well, there is very little point in inviting people to come and see them. Most people have found that shelving is far and away the best answer to the problem, but some collectors have even hung cans from ceilings. Some have piled them high on top of each other in pyramid form, others have stacked them two rows at a time up their stairway. But these ideas are poor substitutes for shelving.

If the collector is a handyman he can put shelves up himself quite cheaply. If he finds such things difficult, the next best solution is to buy good plastic covered metal shelving, which can be erected easily enough and which provides an excellent base on which to place cans. If a little more cash is available, wooden shelving could be put up by a specialist craftsman. One Chicago manufacturer, incidentally, has gone to the trouble of making shelving especially for beer can collectors. It can be bought made and finished, and can go straight

on the wall, ready for the prized cans to be placed on it.

The next question is where to put the shelves in the chosen room. This may cause difficulties as well, but if at all possible, the shelving should be erected around the walls of the room. This allows plenty of space in the middle of the room to stand back and look at them. However, not everybody has enough wall space to cope with a large quantity of cans. One keen collector in Lafayette, Indiana, had over 4,000 cans to put into a very tiny room and it proved quite impossible to fit them all on the walls.

If this solution is impossible, then dividers will have to be used. These are partitions which run across the room from one side to the other and which have shelves on either side. It must be understood that if dividers are used the whole room is going to be turned over to the collec-

83

tion: this cannot be avoided. Obviously space must be left at the end of the dividers for people to walk around.

Dividers have been used successfully by some of the world's great collectors: Ron Moermond is an excellent example. His outstanding collection is situated in just two rooms, one of which is quite small. Nevertheless, he has managed to display many thousands of cans and there is still space to walk from one row of shelving to another and to examine the collection in reasonable comfort.

One last problem arises with the display of party cans. These are after all quite tall and take up a good deal of space. Many collectors display them on the floor around the rooms, beneath the main area of shelving. If this is not possible ordinary shelving must be used, but it will have to be made deep enough to carry these large cans.

Having arranged the shelving in a suitable room, some method must be found of recording the cans in the display – in other words, each collector should have his own inventory. Different people use different systems, but basically they all record each brand of can by its trade name and by the name of the manufacturing brewer. It is also useful to record the sizes of the cans in stock.

A new collector should buy a book or set of filing cards in which to keep an index of each can by name. There should also be a separate index of brewer's names. Occasionally, the same brand of beer is issued by two separate brewers (after a merger for example) and by using this type of cross reference the different specimens may be included in the collection.

Breaker Malt Liquor is a good example of this. One of Britain's two malt liquors, Breaker has been issued in a whole variety of cans and if it were recorded under name only, a second or subsequent specimen would not be accepted for the collection. If Breaker is cross checked under brewer's name, however, different specimens could be accepted marked 'Brewed in the UK by Bass Charrington Ltd London', 'Brewed by Tennent Caledonian Breweries Ltd Glasgow Scotland' or 'Brewed in the UK by Bass Charrington Ltd Burton on Trent'.

Further indexing may be used to record which cans in stock are in steel, or aluminum; or are straight sided or crimped. These structural differences between cans of the same brand are of some significance to the serious collector, so a sensible method must be found to record what is in stock.

Some collectors also record how they obtained the can – whether they bought it empty or full; if they traded it, from whom they got it. This information is of sentimental value, but of little use otherwise and is probably best avoided.

Many collectors collect every size of can available and it is very important to note against the brand in the record system in what sizes it is held, so that others may be collected as they become available. An example of this is Double Diamond, which is made in Britain in three sizes: 275 ml, 330 ml and 440 ml. The design on each is the same but the size is demonstrably different and each is therefore a different can to the serious collector.

It is a moot point whether metal differences should be displayed. This is up to the individual collector, but inasmuch as aluminum differs from steel, so the cans also differ and there is a very strong case for displaying them all. Collectors who only keep one example of each brand name are not really collecting different cans, merely different brands – which is another matter altogether.

Keeping a record system up to date is not the

easiest thing in the world and this should be acknowledged. Nevertheless a proper inventory is essential and it *must* be kept up to date, otherwise it soon loses its value. It is a pity that everybody cannot do what collector Professor D. R. Kurtz does, and maintain his records each day on a computer. Now that is luxurious collecting indeed!

When a new collector has a room chosen, the first shelf built and the record book open all that remains is to get the first can! This is where collecting suddenly becomes a reality and in many ways getting the cans is the easiest part of collecting. Cans may be bought in the shops and the contents drunk. This is a good way of starting off.

Remember that when full cans are bought they should be turned upside down and emptied by punching two holes through the bottom. This means that the rip top is left on and when the can is placed on a shelf it appears to be an unused, or 'virgin', can. It looks much nicer displayed in this way.

Then comes a point when one has obtained all the different brands and brand variations that are available locally through normal retailers. Now one must look further afield, not forgetting that new designs are always appearing and that new brands will be available in local shops from time to time. One needs to keep one's eyes open constantly.

Next one should try to trade or exchange any

The author with one of America's leading collectors, Ken Zent of Fort Wayne, Indiana

Another example of a beer
can with several changes
of label

opposite
Five different designs — but
they're all Guinness

Two American oddities: a cup for the Cornell University reunion, and a drinking can for Princeton made by Budweiser

duplicate cans with those of other collectors. Of course, the rarer the cans one has to swap the better the chance of obtaining good cans in exchange. Common cans will normally trade one to one. There are always collectors starting up who have quite common cans from distant areas which they are anxious to trade for your locals, so there is never any need for the collector to despair.

It is important to observe certain rules in trading, particularly by post or over the telephone. Firstly, agree the basis of the trade. A scarce but current can, or a foreign can, may be worth two of yours. A foreign can that is in demand may be worth five of your stocks. A party can should be worth ten fairly common cans, while highly valued specimens like 007 or Gretz's cars may be worth even 100 cans.

The basis of the exchange can only be decided by sensible discussion and by asking the advice of other collectors, who may be more knowledgeable than you are. Never take just one person's word for a can value: he may want to do you out of a good deal! Remember that values change quickly as inflation bites or as particular designs command popularity— consultation with a fair and experienced collector will reap many benefits.

If you are unable to find the can you want in a trade, you will have to consider buying it. The problem is to know where to go. Flea markets and secondhand or antique shops are best avoided unless the vendor is generally knowledgeable about cans. There are two sound alternatives.

First, another collector may be willing to sell you the cans you want if you do not have any trading stock that he needs for his collection.

If so, well and good. If he cannot help you, go to a specialist dealer who is well known and has a good name for fair dealing. Before you make such a visit find out the current value of the can you want, so that you will not be asked for some inflated price. There are a number of good dealers in the United States, and one or two in other countries, whose knowledge and prestige you may rely on.

Always go to a dealer with whom you have recourse in the event of the transaction falling through. This is particularly important in buying through the mail. Only go to a name which is known for its personal integrity. All the major dealers advertise regularly in the various beer can collectors' magazines that are published.

If the can you are looking for is very old you may have to go out dumping–that is, looking for it in old buildings and rubbish dumps. You may decide that this is a good thing to do in any case. Some quite fantastic finds have been made by searching this way.

When you do find cans, a major problem may be the condition in which you find them. Many may be marked or scratched or even rusted. In that case you are going to have to do a certain amount of restoration or preservation. This is quite an art and some collectors have developed very real skills in pursuing it. Do remember first of all that a can is only worth repairing if the great bulk of its shell remains. Containers that are simply pieces of rust hanging together are just not worth working on.

Starting with cans in mint condition, first remember not to keep them in a damp room, for this would be bound to cause rust. Once rust sets in it is difficult to do anything about it. Next, if you want to put some preservative on the cans, a good wax spray will not do any harm and may well help to keep rust away. A vinyl spray can also be used to preserve the outside appearance. This sort of thing is very much a matter of personal choice; it is not strictly speaking necessary and some major collectors insist that all cans need is a good dusting now and then. Certainly they will come to little harm providing that the room they are kept in does not get damp.

If your cans are rusty, pitted or dented, you will have to try to improve their appearance. Do not forget that you can make the situation worse as well as better if you are over zealous in your endeavours! Rust can only be treated, never cured. What rust has already corrupted cannot be saved and to replace a portion of the can with another piece of metal is not restoring it to its original condition.

If the can is severely rusted, throw it away, for it will only detract from the other cans around it in the display. If there are only spots of rust, they can be removed by rubbing them gently using emery paper, but it is the easiest thing in the world to remove good parts of the can at the same time.

Dortmunder Union Special 500 ml, Schlitz Tallboy ¾ US quart (US), Pabst Blue Ribbon quart (US), Eldridge Pope's Huntsman Homecan 7 pint (3·86 litres) (UK), Schlitz Malt Liquor 8 oz (US)

Another look at Ken Zent's impeccable display

There has been huge correspondence in magazines about the wisdom of using oxalic acid; this certainly does remove rust, but whether it is the best solution is a matter of speculation. Once rust has been removed the paint work may be touched up with paint made for cars if the colors can be matched. But this kind of work requires skill and a very steady hand, and the end result will never be better than second best.

If dents are the problem, there are a host of possible solutions. Many dents may be 'popped out' by carefully pressing the area around the can. Several collectors have removed dents—even from party cans—by filling them with water and putting them in the refrigerator: the water when frozen expands and presses out the dent. Be careful that the can does not expand too much. Air pressure can also be applied to dented cans, and this works quite well.

If the can does not have a bottom, or if the bottom is removable, the problem is far easier to cope with. Careful work with your hands or with a blunt-ended tool will do wonders. If the container then needs a new bottom, you will find someone to do this if you watch the small ads in collectors' magazines. The cost is not too great and the job is easily and quickly done.

Do remember when trading to specify clearly what work, if any, has been done on a can, for trading is largely a matter of good faith and personal integrity. In arranging a postal trade cans must be described accurately. You would not like to get a grade five can when you were expecting it to be mint. If the can is rusty or otherwise damaged, say so. Try hard to qualify its value accurately: a repaired can that looks mint is not as valuable as a mint one. A can that has been repaired is clearly not as good as a grade two unrepaired can. Be fair and describe the container as it is and you should trade successfully.

When posting cans, remember that they are fragile and will not travel well if packed loosely or in thin boxes. Never do what one foolish novice did—send the can through the post unwrapped with an addressed label stuck to it! Always use strong cardboard boxes like the ones spirits are shipped in, and plenty of packing material. Wrap each can individually in newspaper and pack them tightly against each other so that they do not move around in transit. Always attach two labels to the parcel in case one comes off. If the cans are packed this carefully you will be astonished how well they travel. Good packing really does pay.

When friends go abroad ask them to send or bring back some empty cans for you. Pay them to drink the local brews on your behalf so that they have a real incentive! Brief them on what cans to look for overseas and tell them which foreign beers are already in your collection so that they won't bring back specimens you already have—nothing can be more annoying than that.

Have a visiting card prepared with your

opposite and left
7-Up's contribution to the Bi-Centennial : a can for each of the United States. Pile them up to see Uncle Sam

name, address and telephone number. Give it to every collector you meet so that they remember you and call you when they are in your area. Give the card an original theme, if you can think of one, so it stands out from the many others that collectors give to each other. Have your friends and fellow collectors visit your house for a beer as much as possible so that they get into the habit of saving cans for you and bringing them round.

It is important to draw up a trading list as soon as you have enough spare cans to start trading. The sooner you have a trading list the sooner other collectors will want to exchange cans with you. It should be kept up to date just as meticulously as your inventory, since it will be referred to by other collectors. There is no point in your offering something on your list which you have already exchanged with somebody else. Of course, with the best will in the world no-one can keep pace with minute to minute changes.

By the time you have done all this you will rightly begin to feel quite an established collector. You will have found many new friends and will have gained something of a reputation. In fact, if you are lucky, your local paper may want to run a feature especially about you and your hobby. Certainly, if you get as much pleasure out of your new hobby as 50,000 others have done you will be a very happy person. In fact, you will be agreeing with the 10,000 members of Beer Can Collectors of America that 'Beer cans are beautiful'. As indeed they are!

following page
A selection of beer cans in different shapes and sizes

A hobby the kids can enjoy ? Quosh Jokers Orangeade (UK)

Acknowledgments

The publishers would like to thank the following persons who have kindly allowed their collections to be photographed for this book:

William B. Christensen, Madison, New Jersey; Richard R. Dolphin, Bridgwater, Somerset; Pinchas Jaspert, London.

The photographs in this book were taken specially for the Hamlyn Group by Derek Balmer with the exception of the following:

Alcan International 41; Courage Ltd, Reading 18; R. R. Dolphin, Bridgwater 27, 28 top, 29 top left, 29 top right, 30 top right, 44 left, 46 top, 47 top left; Hamlyn Group–Eric Pollitzer 16 top left, 19, 24 bottom left, 24 bottom right, 25 top, 25 bottom, 42, 44 right, 46 bottom, 61 top; I.C.I. Ltd, London 40; W. P. Jaspert, London 8, 23, 28 bottom right; King Features Syndicate Inc., New York 89 top; Metal Box Ltd, Reading 7, 28 bottom left, 29 bottom, 30 bottom, 32–33, 37, 69 top; News-Sentinel, Fort Wayne, Indiana endpapers, 84–85, 90–91.

Index